GAINING POWER
THROUGH PRAYER

Other Books by S. Richard Nelson

Turning Faith into Power

The Added Power of Obedience

The Healing Power of Forgiveness

The Mighty Power of the Word

The Gift and Power of the Holy Spirit

Love: The Only True Power

Sustainable Spirituality

The Faith Factor

This Is Life Eternal

5-star reviews are a blessing to Christian authors. If you find this book inspirational, educational or simply enjoyable, please post an honest review.

The Powerful Christian Series - Book II

GAINING POWER
THROUGH PRAYER

By S. Richard Nelson

First Edition published 2012
Second Printing 2013
Third Printing 2019

ISBN-13: 978-0-9852470-2-7
ISBN-10: 0985247029
BISAC: Religion / Christian Life / Spiritual Growth

Broken Hill Publications
Glenwood Springs, CO 81601

Artistic Design by Connie Gorton
Edited by Stephen Gorton

"From this broken hill,
All your praises they shall ring."

L. Cohen – If It Be Your Will

www.srnelson.com

"For God did not give us a Spirit of fear but of power and love and self-control."

2 Timothy 1:7 (NET)

Table of Contents

INTRODUCTION 13

THE POWER OF PRAYER 15

THE ENABLING POWER OF GOD 27

THE MIRACLE OF PRAYER 35

THE PROMISE OF PRAYER 47

A SPIRITUAL POWER-LINE 61

FINDING PEACE THROUGH PRAYER 69

OTHER BOOKS BY S. RICHARD NELSON 78

EXCERPT: 82

"Our prayers may be awkward. Our attempts may be feeble. But since the power of prayer is in the one who hears it and not in the one who says it, our prayers do make a difference.

Max Lucado

Introduction

"Next to the wonder of seeing my Savior will be, I think, the wonder that I didn't make better use of the power of prayer." Amma

Every faithful Christian should be intimately acquainted with the remarkable power of prayer. Sincere prayer is a fountain of divine power flowing into our lives. Through prayer we gain clear and precise direction. Through prayer we access the strength of character to perform God's will – to do what is right. Prayer is the process we use to place ourselves in contact with God.

But do we really recognize the astonishing power of prayer? Can we grasp what a pronounced blessing it is to address our Father in heaven in simple prayer, aware that He is interested in us and wants us to be successful in our day-to-day activities? If we allow it, prayer can be a significant force in our lives.

Every one of us should have a definite conviction of the power of prayer. God has given us His promise; "Ask, and it will be given to you; seek, and you will find; knock, and it will be opened to you. *For every one who asks receives. He who seeks finds. To him who knocks it will be opened.*" (Matt. 7:7-8)

The impressive power of prayer warrants the consideration not only of Christians, but of all societies everywhere. This little booklet will highlight the principle applications and purposes of prayer. It will confirm that God does answer our prayers and demonstrate how we can be more aware of those divine answers. It will also examine the challenging question of why, at times, it appears that God does not answer us.

People often fail to appreciate the actual advantages of prayer. *Prayer is power.* It has an impact that relatively few of us realize. Yet all of us, I believe, could use a little help from the Lord! I pray that the ideas offered in these pages are of true value to all who read them.

Chapter 1

The Power of Prayer

The greatest miracle of all communication is undeniably the awesome power of prayer! It never loses service or drops a call. It never breaks down. It has no "dead zones". We can never go over our minutes. It never limits the number of requests we may offer up in each prayer. It never goes to voicemail. Nothing can disconnect us from direct contact with God. He is reachable at any time and in any place.

God grants us the gratification of conversing directly with Him. He sets no restrictions as to time, place, or substance of our prayers. The Apostle Paul wrote, "*In everything* by prayer and petition with thanksgiving, let your requests be made known unto God." (Philippians 4:6)

Each of us, at times, needs a little help in some aspect of our lives. Perhaps we are facing problems in our families. Maybe we are dealing with work or career issues. We could be undergoing financial difficulties or maybe we are struggling with personal shortcomings and imperfections.

The fundamental secret to success in any of these areas is prayer. Prayer is the source of spiritual power. When we discover how to obtain answers to prayer, we can tap into God's infinite power and goodness to assist us in our troubles. Without the power of prayer, we typically face our problems on our own.

Sincere believers shouldn't need to be encouraged to pray, and yet many do not say formal prayers. They do not consider what it means to their lives when they disregard the gift of prayer. When we fail to pray, we forfeit the promises that prayer tenders. Our lives should be infused with the influence of prayer and gratitude to God. We should never deny ourselves His power by disregarding the power of prayer.

Prayer lifts our thoughts to a higher and nobler plain; and leads our lives to worthier pursuits. It provides passage for the grace and glory of God to pass through and will illuminate, expand, elevate, and bless all those who avail themselves of its power. Prayer's resolute power to transform our souls is unquestionable.

Undoubtedly, gaining power through prayer takes determined effort. Too often we make prayer a matter of convenience instead of an absolute priority.

The late millionaire, William Clement Stone, explains that only if we "have drive, the push, 'the want to' will you succeed in any field..." He then adds, "Regardless of your religious beliefs, read the Bible, the most inspirational book of all time. *And learn to employ the power of prayer.*" Stone knew the value of commitment. He had determination and ambition. He also trusted in God for guidance and support.

Ask yourself these questions: How often and how sincerely do I pray? Do I "hunger and thirst" for answers or am I satisfied with simply voicing a few worn-out phrases and clichés before I jump into bed? How genuinely are my desires, wishes and concerns expressed? Am I indifferent or lazy in my approach? What do I ask God for and how long do I persist before giving up? When I pray, am I just speaking to God, or am I also listening for His answers?

Jesus said: "Behold, I stand at the door and knock. If anyone hears my voice and opens the door, I will come in to him, and will dine with him, and he with me." (Rev. 3:20)

This is a promise made to each one of us! There is no bias or favoritism. He stands and knocks. If we listen, we *will* hear His voice. If we open the door, He *will* come in and dine with us. He *will* answer our prayers. The Lord stands knocking. He never moves away. But we must open the door. He will never force Himself upon us. He won't break down the door. We are responsible for learning how to listen; how to find an answer; how to interpret and understand.

Within God's word we can easily find a promise that fits our need, whatever that need is. We can then go to God and say, "Lord, this is Your word; prove it's so by implementing it in my life. I believe in Your word; now make it happen according to my faith." We can expect a complete fulfillment of every sentence that God has spoken. Oblige the Lord with His own words, and expect Him to do as He has said, simply because He said it.

The promise of Revelation 3:20 is a summons to pray. It is the very substance of prayer. It says that we can approach God and say to Him, "This is Your word, Lord, now do what You said; please fulfill Your promise." This is, in essence, the power of prayer.

We are taught that knowledge is power, but knowledge is really only *potential* power. Unless we act on what we've learned, knowledge is of no worth to us. Power is knowledge coupled with action. When we learn something new, we should make that knowledge operational in our lives.

I want you to write down a request you have for God. It should be something that you desire very strongly. Maybe you're worried about your spouse or concerned about one of your children. Perhaps you struggle with poor health. You could be facing grave financial difficulties. Or possibly you are just looking to increase your faith or to overcome a personal weakness.

Select a worthy objective to pursue in prayer. *Jot down your request and work on it as you move through this booklet.*

As you do, you will discover that the power of prayer is like a ladder between heaven and earth by which we express our wants to God, and God conveys His blessings to us. We present ourselves at the throne of grace, praising God for the promises He provides, and pleading for additional promises on which we can depend. We approach God in prayer because of prayer's inherent assurance that God is waiting and willing to respond.

We are often motivated to pray out of necessity. Abraham Lincoln, a great believer in prayer, said: "I have been driven many times to my knees by the overwhelming conviction that I had nowhere else to go." We should also be drawn to pray simply by the anticipation which God's promise produces. God provides us a reason to pray and then persuades us with kindly assurances of a response. First, we are tested, and then we test His promise to answer our need. We sense a spiritual thirst, and then quench that thirst with the word of God.

Some seem to believe in prayer, but not in the power of prayer. They pray but do not actually expect God to answer them. We must have complete faith in the power of prayer. The prophet Hosea assures us that "The ways of the Lord are right." (Hosea 14:9) God will respond when we make honest petitions and open our hearts to His counsel and guidance.

Since God knows our hearts, when we are alone with Him, we can pray with increased intensity and feeling. We can drop any façade and charade. We can put aside our duplicity and our pride. We can abandon all insincerity and illusory deceit. Jesus went into the mountains alone to pray. Paul found his solitude in Arabia. He started out a worldly man and returned renewed, regenerated and reborn.

Have you ever prayed with similar intensity? Have you ever prayed for an entire day? Have you prayed for an hour or even half an hour? Or do you pray for just ten minutes out of every twenty-four hours?

Our prayers can usually be counted in seconds and yet, with such a paltry effort, we still expect God to answer us with abundance. God asks us to pray "evening, morning, and at noon" (Psalms 55:17), and to "pray without ceasing." (1 Thessalonians. 5:17) We cannot invest pennies in our prayers and expect thousands of dollars in return.

Sometimes we lack the faith that God will hear and answer our prayers. Perhaps we haven't recently recognized a response when we pray. Consequently, our attempts to pray, if we pray at all, become shallow and superficial. We pray, but don't persevere long enough or patiently enough for a reply. We can feel, therefore, that our prayers go unanswered.

Jesus' advice to us regarding the great second coming was to watch, "for you do not know in what hour your Lord comes." (Matthew 24:42) This same advice applies also to the peaceful, quiet moments He comes silently and secretly in answer to our heartfelt supplications.

When we pray, do we order God around, demanding ridiculous blessings we don't really deserve or do we pray for His will in our lives? Do we pray humbly and honestly, or are we like the proud Pharisees telling God how obedient we are? Do we tell Him how worthy we are, or how weak? Do we pray only now and then, when the need arises, or often and consistently? Do we quickly mumble some "vain repetitions" or do we speak directly and intimately with God until we are heard? Do we truthfully make a concerted effort to have our prayers answered?

Addressing God as "Our Father, who is in heaven" instead of addressing some universal consciousness actually effects the influence of our prayers. Praying to an insubstantial god robs us of the expectation and hope that our prayers will receive a compassionate response. Without this faith, we cannot be heard. But we can confidently pray to a God we know and understand with the certainty that our prayers will be heard and answered.

Such a belief is essential to true prayer because rational and sensible people do not pray fervently to a God they do not even know. Fervent prayers are offered only by those who believe their prayers will be heard and answered by an understanding, sympathetic God.

But it isn't just a lack of faith that will stop us from praying. Sin often obstructs our connection with God. As Mark Twain's fictional character, Huck Finn reminds us: "I about made up my mind to pray and see if I couldn't try to quit bein' the kind of boy I was and be better. So I kneeled down. But the words wouldn't come. Why wouldn't they? It weren't no use to try and hide it from Him. . . . I knowed very well why they wouldn't come. It was because my heart wasn't right; it was because I was playin' double. I was lettin' on to give up sin, but way inside of me I was holdin' on to the biggest one of all. I was tryin' to make my mouth say I would do the right thing and the clean thing, but deep down in me I knowed it was a lie and He knowed it. You can't pray a lie."

Although sin often compels us to stop praying, likewise prayer compels us to cease sinning. We can, as Peter said: "Become partakers of the divine nature, having escaped from the corruption that is in the world by lust...he who lacks these things is blind, seeing only what is near, having forgotten the cleansing of his old sins." (2 Peter 1:4, 9)

All of us can learn by observation and study and by reading the philosophies and ideologies shared in books. We gain a greater value, however, from the learning that comes directly from God. It will enlighten our thoughts and enrich our emotions. The messages and teachings from God will have a profound transformational effect on our lives.

This transformation is available to all of us if we humbly and earnestly pursue it. If we ask, God will award us the blessings He wishes to impart. He will give us encouragement, motivation and divine direction in every aspect of our lives.

The purpose of prayer, ultimately, is to give us a new birth and to draw us closer to God.

"The Prayer of a righteous person is powerful and effective."

James 5:16

Chapter 2

The Enabling Power of God

By implementing the power of prayer, we create a way for God to work through us. Now that you have a written objective to work on while reading through this booklet, let's look at the tenet that qualifies us for a resolution to our requests.

Jesus tells us not to be concerned over what we will eat or drink because "your Father knows that you need these things." (Luke 12:30) If God knows what we want even before we ask Him, why should we even need to pray?

While sincere prayer brings the effect of God's power into our lives, much of prayer is egotism, with our own desires, interests, and needs at the epicenter of our supplications. The core of mighty prayer is *not* for God to do our bidding. Rather, it is refining our intentions so that God can accomplish His will through us.

A selfless, God-centered prayer may not lead to worldly privilege, pleasure, or prosperity. It may, instead, help us to do without these things or, at least, to use them as a trusted partner with God. An alliance with God, who can give harmony and guidance to our righteous purposes, should be our greatest desire.

Jesus does not want *just* to save us from our sins. He also wants to assist us with our personal problems; our illnesses, our imperfections, our weaknesses, and our discouragements. In the process He assists us in becoming eligible for the blessings we seek, and that is called grace.

Grace has been described as "an enabling power". It is a divine channel of aid and assistance; of strength, power and stamina; granted through the mercy of Jesus Christ. Grace, in other words, is the enabling power of God.

All the gifts we receive from God are regulated by statutes and stipulations. When we conform to God's decrees and satisfy the stipulations, God *will* reward us. Too often we don't have the aptitude to do everything necessary by ourselves. We pray earnestly and perform persistently but we still can't meet the requirements God dictates. After we have done all we can do, the grace of the Lord will intercede. The enabling power of God will intervene in our lives and the grace of Jesus Christ will provide what we are missing.

Children readily receive answers to their simple yet sincere supplications to God. A child may not understand much of the concept or conditions of prayer, but a child does know how to speak from the heart and that is all that is required. The Lord supplies the rest. This is the reason children seem to have such direct access to the windows of heaven.

We, too, can have the same access to heaven if we will "become as a child" and offer our prayers from the heart. Then, as we do all we can to meet the conditions for the answer we request, Christ will, through the enabling power of God, intervene and bring about the desire of our hearts.

When we work toward the grace of God, Christ will reward our efforts. He will attend to our supplications and answer our prayers. If we do what is required on our part, then assuredly He will fulfill His promise to us. "Let us therefore draw near with boldness to the throne of grace, that we may receive mercy, and may find grace for timely help." (Hebrews 4:16.) This tenet, however, is dependent on the greater knowledge of God. Because He loves us, God will forever grant what is beneficial to us over our own supposed desires.

The Word of God shows us how to achieve grace so Jesus Christ can assist us. Grace comes first by faith. If we possess real faith, nothing doubting, we can obtain grace, which gives us the answers we search for in prayer. Paul wrote: "Being therefore justified by faith, we have peace with God through our Lord Jesus Christ: *through whom we also have access by faith into this grace.*" (Romans 5:1-2)

Faith in God helps us foster a personal love for Him, one that is reciprocated by Him through blessing us in our greatest times of need. God will reward our faith with power to endure and to overcome adversities, frustrations, anxieties, and all the complexities of day-to-day living. With faith in God we will not turn away from His everlasting course nor be dissuaded by the ways or the praise of the world.

In the Book of Mark 11:24, Jesus instructs us that we must first believe, and then we will receive our answer. "Therefore I tell you, all things whatever you pray and ask for, *believe that you receive them, and you shall have them.*" Real faith asserts a belief that our request has already been answered.

Our faith must be centered in Jesus Christ, who has both the power and the desire to answer our sincere supplications. Christ will always look after what is in our best interest. We need only trust that our prayers will be answered according to His holy will.

Sometimes God discloses His answers in intervals, compelling us to exercise additional faith to attain further resolution to our concerns. We must walk to the edge of the light and step a foot or two into the darkness before the answers will be revealed. Until we can take that first step of faith, doing everything we can do and then trusting in God for the rest, we may not be ready to receive additional answers to our prayers.

Grace comes through submission. We do not have to be flawless to obtain grace, but we do have to try to obey God's word as best we can. Then the Lord will permit us to obtain His enabling power.

Grace comes to the repentant heart. A penitent nature is necessary to attain grace. We should discover what we must change in our lives, what sin we need to discard and then do it. God's answers to our prayers may be contingent on remorse and sorrow for sin more than any other condition.

Grace comes through personal effort. Too often we want answers without effort. Until we do our part, the grace of God may not be evident in our lives. All of us make significant choices that shape our existence. We should thoughtfully consider important decisions such as which college to attend, what career to pursue, where to live, whom to marry, and other vital concerns. Once we have explored the various possibilities and done all we are capable of doing ourselves, then we can count on the Lord to intercede. We receive grace, the enabling power of God, after we have done all that we can do to resolve the important issues in our lives.

Grace is not based on who we are, how much we know, or how much faith we have. It is based on our willingness to give all that we can give and do all that we can do according to our current capabilities. We act as if everything depends on us but pray as if everything depends on God. Once we have given all we can, then the Lord, through His grace, will assist us with the rest. Trusting in God and relying on his influence and ability, we gain strength and power to persevere and prevail.

When we do receive answers from God, it is not due to the effort we made. Our efforts do not bring us replies, but they show our true desires. So, we do what we are capable of, and then allow God's grace to do the rest.

Grace comes to the humble. The apostle James wrote that "God resists the proud, but gives grace to the humble." (James 4:6) Humility lies at the focal point of how we see ourselves in our hearts. When we exercise humility toward God and others, grace will come, power will come, and our prayers will be answered.

The important elements, then, which bring answers and power from God are faith, submission, repentance, effort and humility. When we surrender our hearts to Christ in faith and humility, then He will give us His grace. And how much grace can we expect to be given? All that we could possibly need and require because His grace is sufficient for everyone.

The power of prayer is forceful. Its rewards are resplendent. The marvelous wonders wrought by prayer amaze and astound us. They reinforce our faith and encourage our expectation. The righteous and honest request that you've written down, if it is in accordance with God's will for you, will be given to you, provided you comply with the edicts that dictate your request.

"Pray until your situation changes. Miracles happen every day, so never stop believing. God can change things very quickly in your life."

Chapter 3

The Miracle of Prayer

One of the primary purposes of prayer is to place us in divine harmony with God. Sincere prayer is much more than simply sending our words and thoughts heavenward. It is, instead, the yearnings of the devoted inner self in sync with Deity. It is the longing of the humble heart ascending toward a benevolent God. Genuine prayer comprises the unmistakable perception that we are God's children and that He loves us. When we can feel that divine harmony with God, then, and only then, can we experience the miraculous power of prayer.

Examples of the power of prayer urge us to be open and honest in our own prayers. The Bible is a testament to the power of prayer to produce miracles in the lives of true believers. It attests that the power of prayer can persuade God to perform momentous wonders. Even the laws of nature cannot impede God when petitioned in holy prayer.

The regions of death were penetrated by the miracle of prayer and its victims restored to life. Elisha and Elijah asserted the miracle of prayer and conquered the realms of death. Peter by prayer brought Dorcas back to life. Paul surely exercised the power of prayer when he embraced Eutychus who fell from the window the night Paul preached. God has dominion over death, and prayer reaches where God reigns.

Elijah, whom James describes as "a man with a nature like ours," by prayer locked up the clouds and sealed up the rain for three and a half years. By the same mighty power of prayer, he unlocked the clouds and unsealed the rain again. "And he prayed again, and the sky gave rain, and the earth brought forth her fruit." (James 5:17, 18)

The continual pestilences afflicted on Egypt to compel Pharaoh to allow Israel to leave were prompted by the prayers of Moses until, finally, Pharaoh begged Moses, "Pray to your God, that He may also take away from me this death." (Exodus 10:17) The plagues, produced by the power of prayer, were removed by this same power.

"The removal of the plagues in answer to prayer was as remarkable a display of Divine power as was the sending of the plagues in the first instance. The removal in answer to prayer would do as much to show God's being and His power as would the plagues themselves. They were miracles of prayer." [i]

The sick are healed by prayer. Not by callous, unemotional prayer, but by effectual, enthusiastic prayer. As

James tells us, "Pray one for another, that you may be healed. The effective, earnest prayer of a righteous man is powerfully effective." (James 5:16)

In seeking healing from sickness, we should plead also for the absolution of our sins. Acknowledging our faults will lead to peace and tranquility. When we, as true disciples, justified in Christ and walking before God in obedience, offer an earnest prayer, begging for the blessing of God, it will greatly benefit us.

In troubled times nothing is more promising than prayer. We must demonstrate great faith during times of hardship and prayer is the indisputable instrument for gaining and strengthening our faith. Therefore, pray when you are alone. Convey to God the depth of your soul's secret passion. Pray with your husband or wife. Allow the influence of God's virtue to be felt as you lovingly pray with your family. The miracle of prayer will shelter you from sin and shield you from temptation. With your heart so converted to God and his power, your capacity for good will become infinitely immense.

When praying, we cannot count on our own merits for an answer. We don't just say a prayer; we must feel the prayer in our hearts. Our attention should be set, our resolve strong and committed and our faith exerted. We may not encounter spectacular miracles in answer to our daily prayers, but we will encounter ample grace. The goodness and the grace of God will always accompany our sincere prayers.

God truly wants to help us in every facet of our personal lives. The method for obtaining His help, whether in our individual aspirations, our important relationships, our business endeavors, our spiritual growth, or in anything else, is to ask; ask in faith and follow the guidance given. Sadly, too many of us simply don't bother to ask and consequently we don't receive the assistance we could have with our daily challenges. Jesus teaches us that if we ask, *we will receive.* God does not ask us to seek Him in vain.

Too many feel that they are not eligible to receive responses to prayer. They may feel sinful and unworthy. They may feel if they were better people then God would listen to them. We must never think that we're not good enough to receive God's help. God loves each one of us, sinner and saint, and eagerly yearns to answer our petitions and direct us to the fulfillment of our heart-felt pleas.

Sometimes we have the propensity to say prayers but to not actually pray. We need to examine the honest intentions of our heart. Are we truthfully looking to God for direction or for justification to just do what we want? Are we sincerely seeking answers or simply saying a prayer to satisfy our conscience?

Claudius, in Shakespeare's play Hamlet, ceased praying because his heart was not in it: "My words fly up, my thoughts remain below; Words without thoughts never to heaven go." [ii]

Prayer is not the product of speech. We often speak with words that dissatisfy; words that fail to articulate our true emotions. Or we speak with words intended only to impress human hearing. Words seldom reach deep enough into the complexities of our sentiment to be able to convey the hidden longing of our heart. Prayer is a product of the soul. It is the honest yearning of our spirit. Prayer is supplication born in hardship and remorse. It is the heart's purest aspiration breathed with the eloquence that prevails in heaven.

Jesus declared: "These people draw near to me with their mouth, and honor me with their lips; but their heart is far from me." (Matthew 15:8) An acceptable prayer is more than mere words.

A child's prayer is artless and elementary, yet it surpasses in splendor and significance the verbose, elaborate language of the learned. Children talk to God as though they were speaking to a friend. Their language is plain, straightforward and unassuming. They speak to God as though He were with them. Children's prayers ascend directly to heaven because their minds are not littered with doubts or uncertainties.

The statement, "Unless you turn, and become as little children, you will in no way enter into the kingdom of heaven," (Matthew 18:3) is suggestively insightful. Perhaps our prayers will not reach God unless they, too, are childlike in purpose, conviction and sincerity.

When we face any difficult circumstance in life, we should have a prayer in our heart. When we are trying to bless and assist others, we should have a prayer in our heart. When we confront the demanding challenges of each new day, God should be dominant in our hearts and in our minds and He will be if we are honestly attempting to "pray without ceasing". (1 Thessalonians 5:17) Otherwise, we are on our own, hoping that our human effort is enough to resolve our toughest challenges.

James, the brother of Jesus, wrote: "...ask of God, who gives to all liberally and without reproach; and it will be given him. *But let him ask in faith, without any doubting.*" (James 1:5-6) Prayer imparts to us the ability to accomplish what we desire, the insight to solve our struggles, and the aptitude to do our best. We should not approach prayer as a beggar looking for a handout. Its purpose is not to serve us like some magic lamp conjuring up results without effort.

Prayer is not demanding from God whatever we want. Prayer is supplication for whatever is good, appropriate and needful in our lives.

James also teaches us that "faith without works is dead." (James 2:20) We shouldn't expect God to help us lose weight if we continue to eat unhealthy and fattening foods. We shouldn't expect God to help us pass an exam if we fail to prepare through proper study. God will, however, help us learn, study, think, and recall what we have studied.

The implication from James is that we should ask God to bless us with success in our work, but we should also work as hard as we can to bring an answer to that prayer. We should seek intelligence and then attempt to act wisely. We should pray for good health but live a healthy lifestyle and take care of our physical selves. We should ask for knowledge but study diligently from the best books. We should ask God for His protection and then take every precaution to prevent harm.

When we pray, we should pray for our husbands or wives. We should ask God to bless them in all their daily tasks, their journeys, their occupations, in everything they do. We should also pray for our children. No good parent casually sends a child to school without proper apparel to protect against inclement weather. Yet many parents send their kids to school without the safety of a prayer. Prayer will protect our children against exposure to unknown temptations, malicious people, and undiscovered dangers.

Children occasionally grow up with a defiant mindset despite all we try to do for them. Sometimes pronouncing a heartfelt prayer is all a parent has left to offer them. Remember that the earnest prayer of the righteous is powerfully effective. (James 5:16)

We should also plead for forgiveness and for the strength to forgive others. We should pray for forgiveness for all our inadequacies and weaknesses and ask for strength to do better. When we do, God will hear us and will give us strength to become a powerful influence for good.

Paul asks that "petitions, prayers, intercessions, and givings of thanks, *be made for all men*." (1 Timothy 2:1) The Lord will hear our sincere prayers.

Our petitions should be for the ill and infirm. God may not often heal the sick as we would like, but He may give them comfort, relief and power to persevere.

We should implore God to bless the poverty-stricken and disadvantaged, always remembering *our* responsibility to aid and assist them. "And if a brother or sister is naked and in lack of daily food, and one of you tells them, Go in peace, be warmed and filled; and yet you didn't give them the things the body needs; what good is it?" (James 2:15-16)

Paul also asked that we pray "for kings, and all who are in high places." (1Timothy 2:2) The Lord's guidance is critically needed by our local and national leaders. We can persuade them and assistance them if we will pray to God to give them the intelligence to not be influenced by the unwise, the greedy or the malicious. It is our obligation to pray for the leaders of the nation that they may receive divine direction.

Jesus teaches us that we should also pray for our enemies. Our hearts as well as theirs may be pacified through prayer and we may see the good in them. We should pray for our nation's enemies as well as for neighbors, relatives, and anyone we have disagreements with. Jesus advises us to "Love your enemies, bless those who curse you, do good to those who hate you, and pray for those who spitefully use you and persecute you...For if you love those who love you, what reward do you have?...And if you only greet your friends, what more do you do than others?" (Matthew 5:44, 46-47)

The apostle John invites us to pray for our fellow believers. He emphasized how essential it is to love our friends when he said: "We know that we have passed out of death into life, because we love the brothers. He who doesn't love his brother remains in death." (1 John 3:14)

It is obvious that we must pray for all that in God's wisdom we should have. We should definitely pursue all of the gifts of the Spirit. But primarily, we should plead for the company of the Holy Spirit. The ultimate endowment we can obtain in this life is the gift of the Holy Spirit.

The world today lies in sin and suffering. Heart-rending hurt happens to the most innocent people. God is not the cause, nor is He always the preventer, of life's turmoil. God does, however, sustain us and provide us peace and comfort, through passionate prayer. True believers consistently rely on the miracle of prayer for the fortitude to persevere; for the faith and strength to bear the burdens of the life we undertake for God.

"More things are wrought by prayer than this world dreams of."

Alfred, Lord Tennyson

Chapter 4

The Promise of Prayer

All of our most sincere and earnest praying does not give efficacy to prayer. Kneeling before God in silent or fervent prayer with exquisite beauty and eloquence of expression does not bring power to our prayers. It is the honest and unambiguous *answer* to prayer that testifies of God's existence. It confirms that there is a God who is concerned about us and who listens to us when we pray. Nothing proves the existence of God more than honest answers to our prayers.

Unanswered prayers abandon us to doubt and uncertainty. They present no persuasion to the skeptic or the unbeliever. The answer is the vital element of praying. It is the answer to prayer that glorifies God.

The promise of prayer is simple: Ask, and you will receive. God has promised every one of us help in every facet of our lives as well as continual guidance from His Holy Spirit.

Of course, our prayer must be in harmony with the mind of God. As John wrote: "This is the boldness which we have toward him, that, if we ask anything according to his will, he listens to us: And if we know that he listens to us whatever we ask, *we know that we have the petitions which we have asked of him.*" (1 John 5:14-15)

"I pray," say some, "but God doesn't answer me."

"God just doesn't hear my prayers," say others.

Many others lack the answers they desire because they either do not ask, or they ask a couple of times then quit, without really persisting. God seldom gives us answers to questions we don't ask. He hardly ever bestows blessings we don't seek. But His promise is real: if we ask with a sincere heart, we will receive. So why does it so often seem that God doesn't answer our prayers?

Jesus said: "Ask, and it will be given you. Seek and you will find. Knock, and it will be opened to you. For everyone who asks receives. He who seeks finds. To him who knocks it will be opened. Or what man is there of you, who, if his son asks him for bread, will give him a stone? Or if he asks for a fish, who will give him a serpent? If you then, being evil, know how to give good gifts to your children, how much more will your Father who is in heaven give good things to those who ask him?" (Matthew 7:7-11)

Unequivocal answer to prayer is the motivation repeatedly offered in the word of God that urges us to pray. The Bible does not declare, "Ask, and you will be denied. Seek, and you will get nothing." The word of God is definite: "Ask, and it *will* be given you. Seek, and you *will* find." God's promise is to give for the asking.

To ask and be given an answer is Jesus Christ's formula for prayer. Jesus didn't teach, "Ask, and you will be taught self-denial." He doesn't declare, "Ask, and maybe I'll give you something." Jesus' promise to us is that when we ask, the actual intent of our asking will be given. Jesus didn't tell us, "Knock, and some door will be opened." He promises us that the self-same door we knock on will be opened.

Then, to remove all possibility of doubt, Jesus repeats and reiterates the assurance of an answer. "For every one who asks receives. He who seeks finds. To him who knocks it will be opened." (Matthew 7:7-8)

The word of God is abundant with this promise.

"Call to me, and I will answer you." (Jerimiah 33:3)

"He will call on me, and I will answer him." (Psalms 91:15)

James demonstrates how completely and candidly God assures us answers when we do ask: "You lust, and don't have. You kill, covet, and can't obtain. You fight and make war. *Yet you don't have, because you don't ask. You ask, and don't receive, because you ask amiss*, so that you may spend it for your pleasures." (James 4:2-3)

The explanation to receiving answers to our prayers is not found in the "mysterious" will of God. It is found, instead, in how we pray. We ask but seemingly don't receive answers because *we ask amiss*. When a prayer is answered, it is a confirmation that we are praying correctly. Answers to our prayer are the only guarantee that we have truly prayed appropriately.

An unmistakable answer to a prayer is not only gratifying to our hopes; it is also an indication that we are abiding in Christ. Enjoying distinct answers to prayer, not just once or twice in our lifetimes, but every day of our lives, is a definite sign of our essential relationship with Jesus Christ. The Lord tells us, "If you remain in me, and my words remain in you, you will ask whatever you desire, and it will be done to you." (John 15:7)

The promise of prayer resides in the remarkable reality, limitless in its scope, unfathomable in its richness, that God answers every prayer from every living person who sincerely and honestly prays.

God makes so much available to us and we are usually satisfied with so little. When we understand how to attain answers to our invocations and begin to see how prayer works, we can readily receive the countless gifts God has for us.

At times, we may feel that the Lord has refused to answer our prayers or that our petitions are ineffective if our demands are not resolved instantly and in the manner we desire. We may doubt God's love for us, or even question the reality and power of prayer. At these times it is beneficial to our purpose to continue to persistently and assuredly plead our cause with the Lord. We should remember that God's delays are not God's denials.

A definite criterion of our conviction to Christ and perhaps the most challenging component of praying is to be aware of and accept the answers spoken to us in an idea or an emotion. A constant commitment to prayer, accompanied by faithful reading of God's word, allows us to more readily understand the urgings of the Holy Spirit and synchronizes our souls with the Lord. Jesus tells us to "take my yoke on you, and learn from me, for I am humble and lowly in heart; and you will find rest for your souls." (Matthew 11:29)

When feelings of rejection or abandonment appear or we feel that we're just not good enough, we must keep in mind that perfection on our part is not required to receive answers to our prayers. God desires to answer our pleas with abundant blessings and assistance to comfort us daily. The only real requirement is that we ask with real purpose and resolution. It is not enough to just ask once and be done. According to the laws of faith, we must ask until....

Certain conditions must be met if our sincere prayers are to be answered. We must comprehend and observe the basic tenets concerning prayer. We are obliged to remain in Christ, and let His words remain in us. Then whatever we desire, it will be done. (John 15:7)

Our minds must be ready to receive whatever answer God sends to us. We cannot permit our preferences to eclipse God's purposes and perfect will for us. We must ask according to His will and then we will have the petitions we have asked of Him. (1 John 5:14) We should keep His commandments and do the things that are pleasing in His sight and then whatever we ask, we will receive of Him. (1 John 3:22) And finally, we have to believe, then whatever we ask in prayer we will receive. (Matthew 21:22)

God is constant and confirmed in His word to us; He never falters in His promises. If we fail to realize answers to our invocations, the deficiency is in us and never in God. Maybe we simply don't recognize the answers God offers. Perhaps we're not meticulous enough in searching, or maybe we just don't listen to the Lord's response.

When we pray it is a good idea to trust that the Lord will do what is best for us. The soundest advice I have heard in getting our prayers answered is "to ask in our prayer what to say in our prayer." We are taught from Paul's writing to the Romans: "In the same way, the Spirit also helps our weaknesses, *for we don't know how to pray as we ought*: But the Spirit himself makes intercession for us with groanings which can't be uttered." (Romans 8:26) The response to such a prayer may be precise, powerful and immediately perceptible, or it may be subtle, obvious only to the thoughtful, attentive soul.

The Lord performs His best miracles in situations that are the most challenging! We need to have complete faith in the notion that "with God nothing will be impossible." (Luke 1:36-37) We must remember God's own words to Sarah when she questioned His power: "Is anything too hard for the Lord?" (Genesis 18:14)

Most of us are convinced that God can do anything, but we're not so certain that He will do it for us. This uncertainty in unlocking the power of prayer is an obvious explanation why so many prayers seemingly go unanswered. We think our prayers aren't being answered because it isn't God's will. We blame our unanswered prayer on the Lord, when in reality we didn't apply sufficient faith and didn't possess the confidence needed to receive an answer.

We shouldn't fault God when we lack the confidence to receive answers to our prayers. We must learn to have confidence in God and "draw near with boldness to the throne of grace" (Hebrews 4:16) to obtain the answers we seek rather than denouncing God when we don't get answers. When our conviction is weak, we need to plead like the man who brought his son to Jesus to rebuke a "mute spirit" out of him. Jesus told him, "If you can believe, all things are possible to him who believes. Immediately the father of the child cried out with tears, I believe; *help my unbelief.*" Jesus then "rebuked the unclean spirit" and healed his son. (Mark 9:14-29)

Confidence in God comes to those who have faith in Jesus Christ. The Apostle Paul could "preach to the Gentiles the unsearchable riches of Christ... In whom we have boldness and access in confidence through our faith of him." (Ephesians 3:8-12) Confidence in God comes when we honor the Lord: "In the fear of the Lord is strong confidence." (Proverbs 14:26) Confidence in God comes when our hearts demonstrate that we are accepted of Him: "Let's not love in word only, neither with the tongue only, but in deed and truth. And by this we know that we are of the truth, and persuade our hearts before him... if our hearts don't condemn us, we have confidence toward God." (1 John 3:18-21)

Our prayers may seem to go unanswered when God does not answer them to our precise expectations. God will wisely answer our prayers in His perfect way. Answers may come immediately, or we may have to wait days, months or even years. Some prayers will be answered just as we expected. Some answers will be harder to recognize. *But all genuine, earnest prayers are answered.* When we open our hearts and minds to the variety of means by which an answer may come, we more readily receive the Lord's influence in our lives and increase our faith, consequently increasing our ability to obtain answers.

If we received an immediate and certain answer to our prayers every time, it would eliminate our need to apply faith. Perhaps by deferring us or by giving an obscure answer God is teaching us, for the time being, to implement stronger faith in Him.

Faith is like a mustard seed. If we plant the seed of faith in our hearts, it will grow. We will feel swelling emotions as our faith begins to expand and enlarge our souls. Our faith will grow as we accept God's word and allow His Holy Spirit to work in us.

In book one of The Powerful Christian series, *Turning Faith into Power*, we read about attaining faith in Jesus Christ. "Faith in Jesus Christ is more than simply a pronouncement of belief. Faith in Him entails absolute dependence on Him. He has unbounded power and love. There is no earthly dilemma He cannot solve. He suffered all things and knows how to help us overcome our day-to-day conundrums. Faith means trusting in His wisdom when we are confused and uncertain."

For whatever reason, at times it will seem we just don't get an answer to our prayers. When that happens, God will still speak to our soul and convey His love to us. He may deny our petition in our own self-interest, but because He loves us, He will, in some manner, through some method, breathe into our heart and mind and soul the reassurance that He is on our side, working with us, and everything will resolve itself for our good and His glory. He will comfort us while causing us to increase our faith in Him. God purposefully does not always disclose his complete mind to us so that we might truthfully exercise our faith.

God knows our needs before we even approach Him. He sees our situation in eternal conditions, both the immediate and the timeless, and He will provide for each of us individually according to His matchless wisdom. By so doing, He facilitates our efforts to cultivate increased faith in Him. When we patiently wait on the Lord, letting God know that we trust Him when we presumably are refused an answer, He will, little by little, grant us His absolute and definitive comfort and promise that everything will be alright. We will know that our prayer has been heard, that God is aware of our particular set of circumstances, and that He will work out the entire situation.

Some otherwise devoted believers, when their prayers seem unanswered, turn their backs on the Lord in disappointment and resentment. They begin to doubt the practice and the promise of prayer. Others will grow from the event and carry on with greater faith. They realize that no effort of faith and prayer is fruitless or futile, even if the answer they expected is not the answer they received. Instead, they progress and improve in faith and spirituality, and are better prepared to accept God's will in seeking answers to future prayers.

All prayers spoken sincerely and in faith are answered. But sometimes the answer will not be what we want. The answer may be no; not yet; or some similar response. When the answer we receive is not the answer we had hoped for, we should answer back with more prayers, more love toward God and our Savior, more faith and trust, more persistence and importuning, asking continually, unwilling to stop. Then our faith will be compensated. God will always and only do what is best and beneficial for us. We may not always know how God will answer our requests, but we can trust Him to grant the greatest blessing to us.

How do you react when you don't receive the answer you are searching for? Do you become angry? Do you wonder if prayer really works? Or do you trust God and admit that maybe it's not God's will but your own that you are seeking?

If we do all that is in our power and then trust in God to do the rest, God will tell us what we are still lacking. We will know what more we need to do and, as we do it, God will send us our answer. When we give all that is required, then God can respond by doing what is best for us. Then we can expect to see the hand of God in our lives. When we have done all that God requires, we have complete cause to believe that the Lord will intervene and bless us.

As we begin to faithfully and sincerely seek answers to prayer, Satan will do all in his power to stop us. If we're praying for something of personal importance, we can depend on the devil getting involved. He's anxious to prevent us from getting answers and will try to discourage us from praying. He'll concoct any scheme he can to make us doubtful. We should expect it and when difficulties arise, we will discover how much faith we truly have.

When we attract the devil's attention, it's a good indication that what we're doing is God's will. Satan will do his best to ensure we fail. That should tell us that we're doing something that makes a difference and we can increase our faith. If we increase our faith in times of doubt and setbacks, then we have beaten the adversary.

God will also test us when we approach Him in prayer. We should serve and love Him at all times and in every circumstance. We must remain faithful even if it seems we don't receive the answer we expected. Answers often come after our faith is tested, and we must endure through difficulties if we want the answer we look for.

As we practice the principles of prayer and sincerely try to improve our relationship with God, we will recognize that He hears us and that He does answer our sincerely spoken and heartfelt prayers. We will then be better able to perceive the answers when they come.

"God cares deeply about everything that concerns you so feel free to talk to Him about anything."

Chapter 5

A Spiritual Power-line

Prayer is spiritual energy. It is a power-line that brings into practical realization the promises of God. Without the promises of God, prayer is powerless. Prayer and its promises are synergetic. God's promise motivates us to pray while prayer identifies and reveals God's promises.

Peter affirms that God has afforded us "exceeding great and precious promises" (2 Peter 1:4) and it is prayer which makes the promises substantial, valuable and useful. The realization of the promises of God is based on prayer and it is God's promise that makes prayer so inviting.

The promises of God to His children are grand and sublime and exalted. His purposes are eternal. Why are we so deprived in life and so disadvantaged in nature when God's promises are so "exceeding great and precious"? Often, it is because our prayers are too effortless and meager to implement God's purposes or to obtain the possibilities He has promised us.

Spectacular purposes require spectacular praying to realize them. Miraculous promises necessitate miraculous praying to attain them. Only remarkable praying can activate remarkable promises or fulfill remarkable purposes.

Prayer is founded in the purposes and promises of God. It is a submission of self to the Divine. Prayer strengthens God's will in our lives. It may seek relief from the bitter trials of life and the dismay of indescribable suffering in the words, "If it be possible, let this cup pass from me." But it is also enhanced with swift and sweet submission in the words, "Not my will, but yours, be done."

The promises of God to every penitent sinner are likewise indisputable and unfaltering. The broken-hearted sinner who repents and seeks God through prayer is as equally entitled to the divine promises as are the believers who receive answers to their prayers. The promise of pardon and peace was the basis of the prayers of Saul of Tarsus during his days of darkness and distress.

"Seek you the Lord while he may be found," advises Isaiah, "and call you on him while he is near. Let the wicked forsake his way and the unrighteous man his thoughts; and let him return to the Lord, and he will have mercy on him; and to our God, for he will abundantly pardon." (Isaiah 55:6)

The praying miscreant obtains mercy because his prayer is substantiated in God's promise of pardon to remorseful sinners. The penitent obtains hope of forgiveness in the certain promise of mercy to all who seek the Lord in repentance and faith. Prayer always brings pardon to the sorrowful soul.

The greatest possibilities of prayer have seldom been realized. The promises of God are so magnificent to the truly prayerful that it almost staggers our imagination. His promise to answer, and to do and to give *all things whatsoever* is so immense, so enormous and so exceedingly extensive that it can only astonish and amaze us. We stagger at the promises through unbelief. (Romans 4:20)

Actually, God's sacred promises afforded to us through the divine gift of prayer have been diminished by our own lack of faith and our limited thinking concerning God's ability, generosity and abundance. Most of us never see the full effect and benefit of prayer. Prayer has more power to deliver the blessings of God than anything else. God means what He says in all of His promises. God's promises are His own word and He intends to do exactly what He says He will do for the prayerful and faithful. "For He who promised is faithful." (Hebrews 10:23)

We are the ones who have declined to assert ourselves in prayer. The propensity to pray is available by the grace and power of the Holy Spirit, but it demands such a persistent and pronounced effort that it is rare for any one of us to be on real pleading terms with God. But let me reiterate that "The effective, earnest prayer of a righteous man is powerfully effective." (James 5:16) Who can say how powerful and effective such a prayer can be?

The possibilities of our prayers are dependent on the potential of our faith. Prayer and faith go hand-in-hand. Faith constantly prays and prayer continually believes. Prayer is the voice of faith. Faith is the wing of prayer. Prayer asks and faith receives the answer.

God's supreme power is the foundation of powerful faith and powerful prayer. When God's promises are united to our prayers by faith, then "nothing shall be impossible." Persistent prayer is so resilient and powerful that it obtains the promises of God even against the greatest odds. Through his divine promises, God puts all things He possesses into our hands. Prayer and faith put us in possession of His boundless blessings.

Many of us often never really comprehend the pervasive power of prayer until we come across an overwhelming, urgent crisis and discover that we are unable to solve it on our own. Only then do we humbly acknowledge our complete dependency on Him. God wants us to turn to Him in prayer.

He has offered us the gift and promise of prayer and He is pleased with us when we accept it.

There are a variety of reasons why we don't pray more consistently and meticulously. "I just don't have the time," we declare. "I'm too tired." "I have important things to do." "I just don't really believe that prayer will help me." All of these pretexts and excuses for not praying can be resolved if we will just:

1. **Determine to pray.**

We need to make prayer a habit. If we "remain in Christ," then God will definitely answer our prayers. If we have doubts, we need to assess the level and commitment of our faith.

2. **Determine when to pray.**

Oftentimes, we simply need to make some minor lifestyle changes. We may need to get up earlier in the morning or stay up later at night to make time to pray. We can reduce the time we spend playing video games, watching television, or doing other recreational activities. If we are too busy to pray, then we are just too busy. Electing not to pray should never be an option.

3. **Have the faith that our prayers will be heard.**

Sometimes answers will come plainly and effortlessly. Other times we pray and seemingly receive no answer. When this happens, we have the potential to increase our faith by persisting in prayer until the answer arrives. We should never lose faith in prayer or feel that God doesn't answer us, but we should trust in God with the confidence that He will answer our prayers in His perfect way.

The secret is understanding how those answers come. In his inspiring book, *He Touched Me; My Pilgrimage of Prayer*, John Powell proposes five subtle means God employs to answer us: "Can God put a new idea directly and immediately into my mind? Can God put new desires into my heart, new strength into my will? Can He touch and calm my turbulent emotions? Can He actually whisper words to the listening ears of my soul through the inner faculty of my imagination? Can God stimulate certain memories stored within the human brain at the time these memories are needed?

"If the answer to these questions is yes, then God has at least five channels through which He can reach me, five antennae in my human anatomy through which He can 'touch' me.... I feel sure that God can and does reach us in these ways."

We should never doubt or disbelieve that God answers prayer. He will not forsake His children. God desires to answer our prayers and to honor our worthy petitions. He allows us and expects us to pray for anything appropriate, whether material or spiritual.

Closeness to God is developed through prayer. We needn't concern ourselves with gracious and elegant speech. We should just talk to our concerned and loving Father. We are His cherished children whom He loves perfectly and desires to assist and to succor. He is listening. There is pleasing communion with God through prayer. The inner soul is nurtured and nourished by prayer. There is a sweet, rich and strong delight of God in prayer.

Homer W. Hodge stated: "Prayer should be the breath of our breathing, the thought of our thinking, the soul of our feeling, and the life of our living, the sound of our hearing, the growth of our growing."

Our faith in Jesus and our determination to pray fervently will combine to create abundant power in our lives. If we encourage and build up those attributes, we will gain a greater longing to align our will with the will of God and we'll see our righteous requests become reality.

"Choosing to talk to God with full purpose of heart and mind will transform your prayer experience

S. Richard Nelson

Chapter 6

Finding Peace through Prayer

We can approach God anytime and anywhere. He assures us tranquility in times of trouble and offers a way for us to draw nearer to Him in our need. We can express to Him the simple considerations of our intellect or the unfathomable feelings of our soul. God grants us the privilege and power of prayer. He invites us to "pray always" and promises to pour out His Spirit on us with the blessing of peace given through the miraculous power of prayer.

With extreme sorrow Jesus kneeled in Gethsemane prior to his crucifixion. Knowing that with God all things are possible, He implored: "My Father, if it is possible, let this cup pass away from me: nevertheless not what I want, but what you want." (Matthew 26:38-39) In anguish, sorrowful and so severely troubled that he fell on his face, Jesus prayed three separate times, "Father, if you are willing, remove this cup from me. Nevertheless, not my will, but yours, be done." (Luke 22:42)

God knew what had to be done and so permitted His Beloved Son to suffer for you and me and all humanity. But He did not leave Jesus to grieve alone in his unspeakable agony. Although He accepted Jesus' suffering, God also sent him comfort when "an angel from heaven appeared to him, strengthening him." (Luke 22:43)

When we can trust our Father in heaven and submit to His will as did our Savior, then genuine peace and serenity will fill our hearts, confirming that God has heard and answered our prayers. When we defy God's answers and deny His inspiration then we are denied the comfort, strength and peace that He promises us.

All of us encounter uncertainties. All of us grapple with our share of sorrow, our times of trouble, our portion of problems and our ration of regrets. We face illness and accidents, failure and disappointment, discouragement and depression, the death of loved ones, and other uninvited infringements on our plans and purposes.

But we are not alone. When our troubled temperaments and tangled thinking, our weary wandering and obstinate illnesses, our gnawing doubts and disbeliefs demand higher help than humanly possible, we have the nourishing, nurturing power of prayer. "Call to me, and I will answer you, and will show you great things, and difficult, which you don't know." (Jerimiah 33:3)

Jesus definitely comprehends all of the struggles and difficulties that we undergo. He expects us to offer up our petitions to God in prayer. If we are persistent, our prayers will be answered, our worries will weaken, our doubts will disappear, our misery will melt away, and we will feel God's love and the comfort of his Holy Spirit.

Prayer gives us reassurance and a clearer view of the resolution to the difficulties of the day. In every problem of every passing day, at home or at work or at school, in any family, through any illness and in all our activities, the power of prayer can be an edifying and vitalizing influence; the basis of understanding and a source of truth; a curative and restoring power; a reassurance and a shelter; a fount of peace. Prayer is the ladder we climb to God whose endless power assures us that despite all our disappointment and dismay, all our problems and perplexities, we are not alone in life.

In the memorable narrative, *The Count of Monte Cristo*, Alexandre Dumas wrote, "For the happy man prayer is only a jumble of words, until the day when sorrow comes to explain to him the sublime language by means of which he speaks to God." [iii]

God's word fully confirms the possibilities and extensive nature of prayer. "Call on me in the day of trouble; I will deliver you, and you will honor me. (Psalms 50:15) It doesn't matter how varied our troubles are, how hopeless their influence, how immeasurable their magnitude or how terrible our circumstances! The power of prayer is grander than any trouble, more far-reaching than the depths of any sorrow, more influential than all our agony. Prayer eases all the harm which plagues our lives. Prayer can wipe away any tear. It can elevate any misery and dispel any despair.

God promises: "He will call on me, and I will answer him; I will be with him in trouble; I will deliver him, and honor him." (Psalms 91:15) Prayer brings God and His goodness to our aid. It conveys wonderful revelations of His miraculous power. With God, nothing will be impossible and, all the possibilities that exist through God are revealed in prayer.

The power of prayer reaches to every concern we have, whether physical, material, or spiritual. Prayer answers the tiniest cares of life. It enfolds all our wants and needs. Everything which belongs to this life; health, food, careers, education, finances, as well as all the eternal interests of our hearts is covered by prayer. Its fulfillment is seen in the grand and marvelous miracles of the universe as well as in the trifling tears of a saddened soul.

Our earthly concerns comprise a large part of our lives. They create our strongest stresses and anxieties. Our worldly problems affect our health, our happiness, and our relationships. Prayer invites God into this expansive realm of our existence. We should "pray in everything" because that is the genuine value of prayer. Both our physical needs and our spiritual needs are reliant on God, and prayer is the articulation of that reliance.

Prayer is essential in our lives. Through prayer we place ourselves in harmony with the divine and in tune with the infinite. Prayer is our access to spiritual power. Without prayer, our spirit is starved and our faith withers and dies.

The world stands on the edge of destruction. The profound power of prayer is sadly unused and unfamiliar. Prayer, an indispensable function of the spirit, should be fervently observed. The disregarded discipline of impassioned prayer must be asserted again. If the power of prayer is practiced again, if our spirit can pronounce its purposes plainly and confidently, then our prayers for a sounder and safer world may yet be answered.

God invites us; "Come now, and let us reason together". (Isaiah 1:18) That is His invitation to us. We should develop our faith in the power of prayer. We should pray with an expectation of an answer. Believe in the power of prayer. It is real.

Never underestimate the power of prayer and its miraculous influence.

5-star reviews are like a blessing sent from heaven for Christian authors. If you found this book to be inspirational, uplifting or simply enjoyable, please post an honest review.

About the Author

Rich Nelson is the author of a variety of published articles on topics such as religious education, family values, health, and politics. His work has appeared in *Christian Education Today, Church Teacher, Parish Teacher, Living with Teenagers, Liberty Magazine,* and many others.

Contact Information:

Broken Hill Christian Publications
Glenwood Springs, CO 91601

Email Rich at: rich@srnelson.com

Visit Rich at: www.srnelson.com

Other Books by S. Richard Nelson

Turning Faith into Power:

Book 1 of The Powerful Christian Series.

Turning Faith into Power is the first in a series of instructive and inspirational e-books from The Powerful Christian Series by S. Richard Nelson. The Savior says in Matthew 17:19-20, "For most assuredly I tell you, If you have faith as a grain of mustard seed, you will tell this mountain, move from here to there, and it will move; and nothing will be impossible to you."

What mountains would you remove from your life if you had the faith of a mustard seed? What's stopping you from removing the obstacles in your life? Do you utilize your faith as a principle of action and power? Is your faith centered where it will be most effective? Do you have adequate faith in yourself?

As believing Christians there is substantial power available to us. It is the power of faith. Through the bounteous mercy and love of Jesus Christ we receive his grace - a divine means of strength. The power available to us through Jesus Christ is very real.

Excerpt from

The Added Power of Obedience

Book 3 in
The Powerful Christian Series

by S. Richard Nelson

available at www.srnelson.com

Excerpt:
The Added Power of Obedience

The idea of obedience is a concept not eagerly accepted in today's society. Its appeal and popularity have essentially diminished, but not without reason. Satan has distorted the notion of obedience in order to add to our suffering. Many people have committed tremendous abuse by obeying unethical and immoral leaders. Others have been deceived into espousing evil objectives and have suffered the effects of blind submission.

Genuine obedience never has been blind faith. Rather, it is observing the edicts evident only through the eye of faith. We do not obey because we are blind, we obey because we see. Obedience is so essential to God's designs and purposes for us that we must reclaim it from irresponsible reasoning and inaccurate interpretation.

Obedience is a vital part of the plan of eternal happiness. No criterion is more critical to our well-being in this life or in the next. The ancient prophets and countless Bible verses all teach obedience to God's law.

Greatness is always achieved through obedience.

It is an undeniable declaration from God that everyone who is born will die. "When you eat from it you will surely die." (Genesis 2:17) Not a single one of us will escape death. But that is not the end of our existence. Our souls will continue to exist eternally.

Jesus was born with a mortal body. He was crucified but was raised from the tomb. He severed the clutches of death and rose to a newness of life. You and I must do the same. (See 1 Corinthians 15:22) We will go through the same process in order to access the glory God intended for us. We will rise from the tomb just as Jesus did. This is the purpose of our existence here.

Obedience to the laws of God is fundamental to that purpose. Stability, unity and purpose would not exist without obedience. Obedience increases faith and grants us access to the blessings of heaven. Rebelliousness produces only sorrow and despair.

What God is telling us is, "You forfeited My glory by intentionally disobeying Me. Now you must repent and stop doing things your way. I will give you another chance to regain My glory by willfully and implicitly obeying Me. Simply live by My law of obedience and start doing things My way."

Our submission must be deliberate and intentional; it cannot be obligatory. God will never constrain us against our will. We must obey because we want to, because we have faith, and because we desire to please God. God always welcomes the willing soul.

The dominating ideology that links us with limitless power is the law of faith. Through our faith we attain abilities beyond our reach. The mind acts by reason, the spirit acts by faith.

Without faith, what proof is there that God even exists? Ancient traditions, sacred texts, and miraculous occurrences, however real they may be, are still only intellectual evidences and can always be contested. But through faith, the channel between God and man, the circuit of truth is established. Emerson declared, "Our instinct is trust".

As we obtain a spiritual knowledge of God and begin to understand the things of God, then the counter law is put into operation. Our knowledge of God makes us responsible to Him and invokes *the law of Justice.* His love for us brings us grace under *the law of Mercy* and we become debtors to him, and subject to *the law of Obedience.*

In this chain of laws each link is dependent upon the others, "For the one who obeys the whole law but fails in one point has become guilty of all of it." (James 2:10) If one link is broken, then the entire chain is ruined. If I, knowing the laws of God, disobey them, then I will face justice. If I obey the law, then I will obtain grace, mercy and the blessings of God.

Our individual freedom is dependent on the condition of obedience. This is the great dichotomy; we are free, and yet we are restrained. "Take my yoke on you," said Christ, "and you will find rest for your souls." (Matt. 11:29)

We are free through Holy edict but become subservient to true doctrine by Divine decree. In trading this life for eternal life, we barter obedience for all we own. If we want physical power, we must obey the laws of proper eating and exercise. If we want financial power, we must obey the laws of economy. If we want mental power, we must obey the laws of study and correct thinking. If we want spiritual power, then we must obey the laws of God.

How do we reconcile the difference between these two conflicting ideas? Every one of us, no matter who we are, is restrained by countless cords, and eventually we learn that true freedom is found not in defiance but in obedience to righteous law.

I do not know of a higher law than obedience.

Everywhere throughout the world today we see signs of disintegration, disorder, and anarchy. We lack the cohesive qualities and moral principles that hold our society together. A dearth of love for one another and a disregard for law are slowly breaking down the orderly procedure of civilized society.

Obedience was the leading characteristic and the fundamental principle of power of all the ancient prophets. We must recognize that this same source of power is accessible to all of us today.

Read more of *The Added Power of Obedience* at:

www.srnelson.com

[i] *Possibilities of Prayer*. E. Bounds
[ii] *Hamlet* (Act III, sc. 3). Shakespeare, William
[iii] *The Count of Monte Cristo*, Dumas, Alexandre. Bantam Books 1981, p. 34

www.ingramcontent.com/pod-product-compliance
Lightning Source LLC
Chambersburg PA
CBHW070545030426
42337CB00016B/2357